By T.P Just

~~~

Get All The Books In The Series:
Animal Peculiarity Volume 4 Part 1 [1-3]
Just enterprises

I0425420

Table of Contents

Prologue

1. The Purple Shellfish
2. Birds of India
3. The Mynah
4. The Adjutant Stork
5. The Hoopoe of India
6. A Brahmani Myth
7. The Pangolin
8. The Sand-partridge
9. Water-snakes of India
10. The Indian Mule
11. Monkeys of Prasiaea
12. The Yak
13. Fishes of India
14. The Skate and the prawn of India
15. The Turtle and the Tortoise of India
16. The Ants of India
17. The Chasm of Pluto

Prologue

THERE is perhaps nothing extraordinary in the fact that man is wise and just, takes great care to provide for his own children, shows due consideration for his parents, seeks sustenance for himself, protects himself against plots, and possesses all the other gifts of nature which are his. For man has been endowed with speech, of all things the most precious, and has been granted reason, which is of the greatest help and use.

Moreover, he knows how to reverence and worship the gods. But that dumb animals should by nature possess some good quality and should have many of man's amazing excellences assigned to them along with man, is indeed a remarkable fact. And to know accurately the special characteristics of each, and how living creatures also have been a source of interest no less than man, demands a trained intelligence and much learning. Now I am well aware of the labour that others have expended on this subject, yet I have collected all the materials that I could; I have clothed them in untechnical language, and am persuaded that my achievement is a treasure far from negligible. So if anyone considers them profitable, let him make use of them; anyone who does not consider them so may give them to his father to keep and attend to.

For not all things give pleasure to all men, nor do all men consider all subjects worthy of study. Although I was born later than many accomplished writers of an earlier day, the accident of date ought not to mulct me of praise, if I too produce a learned work whose ampler research and whose choice of language make it deserving of serious attention.

1. The Purple Shellfish

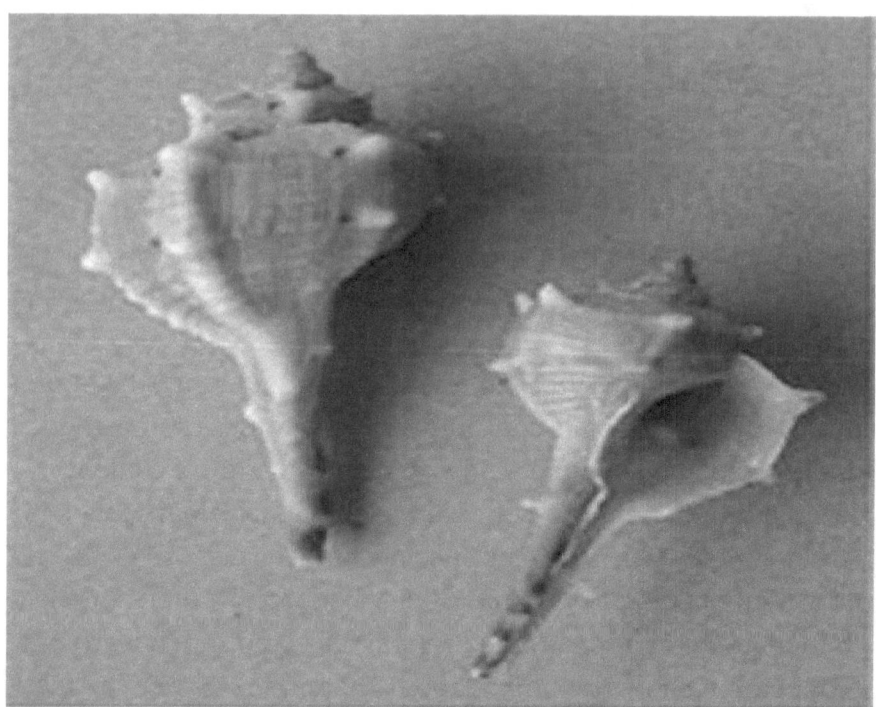

When a fisherman after Purple Shellfish catches one, not for
human consumption but for dyeing wool, if the colour from it
is to remain fast indelible, and capable of producing the
genuine tint unadulterated, then he smashes it, shell and all,
with one blow of a stone.

But if the blow is too light and the creature is left still alive, a
second blow with the stone renders it useless for dyeing
purposes.

For the pain causes the fish to spend the dye which is
absorbed into the mass of flesh or escapes in some other way.

And this, they say, was known to Homer who says of those who die all at once that they are overtaken by the death of the Purple Shellfish: in his poem he sings in the well-known passage how

2. Birds of India

I learn that in India there are Parrots, and I have also
mentioned them earlier on, but this seems a most fitting place
to relate what I did not relate on the former occasion. I am told
that there are three kinds, and all learn like children and
become talkative in the same way and speak like human
beings.

In the forests however they utter the notes of birds, and do not
produce intelligible and distinct speech, but are unlearned
and cannot talk as yet. There are also Peacocks in Indian larger
than anywhere else, and Doves with green plumage; anyone
seeing them for the first time and not possessing knowledge of
birds would say that they were parrots not doves.

But they have beaks and legs the same colour as those of partridges in Greece. And the Cocks, there are of immense size, and their combs are not scarlet like those of our country, but of variegated hue like flower-garlands.

And their tail-feathers are not arched or curved in a circle but flat, and they trail them, just as peacocks do when not raising them aloft. And the wings of Indian Cocks are golden with the dark gleam; of an emerald.

3. The Mynah

There is also in India; another bird, the size of a starling, and it is of varied colouring, and. if taught to utter human speech is more talkative and by nature more intelligent than the parrot. Yet it does not willingly endure to be kept by man, but in its yearning for liberty and its desire for its natural freedom it welcomes starvation in preference to captivity with its luxuries.

And the Macedonians who settled in India in the cities founded by Alexander, the son of Philip, in Bucephala and the surrounding country, in Cyropolis and the rest, call the bird Cercion (mynah).

The name has its origin in the fact that it too wags its rump (cercos) as the wagtail does.

4. The Adjutant Stork

I have heard that there is also in India a bird called the 'Adjutant'. It is three times the size of a bustard, and has a mouth of astonishing size and long legs.

It also has an enormous crop resembling a wallet and an extremely harsh cry.

While; the rest of its plumage is of an ashen colour, the wing-tips are pale.

5. The Hoopoe of India

I have heard also that the Indian Hoopoe is twice as big as the bird of our country and more beautiful in appearance.

And as Homer says that the bit and trappings of a horse are laid up to be a Greek king's glory, so the Hoopoe is the joy of the Indian King: he carries it on his hand and delights in it, gazing continually in wonder at its splendour and its natural beauty.

6. A Brahmani Myth

Now the Brahmins also relate a legend regarding this bird, and the legend they relate is as follows. A son was born to an Indian king and he had brothers who, when they were grown to manhood, became extremely lawless and violent.

And they looked down upon their brother, as being the youngest, jeered at their father and mother, and showed no respect for their old age. Accordingly the parents refused to live with them and departed exile, the, aged couple with their young son.

There ensued a laborious journey for them; the parents' strength failed, and they died. The son however did not neglect them but split his head with a Sword and buried them in himself.

The Brahmins assert that the all-seeing Sun was so filled with admiration for this surpassing act of piety that he transformed the boy into a bird most beautiful to behold and endowed with length of days.

And from his crown there sprang up a crest, as it were in commemoration of the events of his exile. The Athenians too tell-some such wondrous tale in a myth regarding the Lark, which Aristophanes, the writer of comedies, appears to me to have followed in his Birds when he says.

No, for you were unlearned and no busybody and had not thumbed your Aesop, who used to say that the Lark was the first of all birds to be born, before the earth, and that then its father fell sick and: died.

But there was no earth, and the corpse was laid out for five days, and the Lark in straits and at its wits' end buried its father in its own head.

So it seems that this fable from India, about a different bird indeed, yet spread to the Greeks as well.

For the Brahmins maintain that it is long ages since the Indian Hoopoe, while still a human being and a child: in years, did this to its parents.

7. The Pangolin

In India there is an animal somewhat like the land-crocodile in appearance.
It is the size of a Melitean a lapdog. The scales that cover it are so rough and of such close texture, that when flayed they perform the functions of a file.
They will even cut through bronze and eat their way through iron. They call the- creature Phattage (pangolin).

8. The Sand-partridge

The Sand-partridge occurs in the neighborhood of Antioch in Pisidia and feeds on stones. It is smaller than the partridge and black in colour, but its beak is red.

It is not to be domesticated like the partridge, nor does it grow tame but continues wild all the time. It is not large, but is pleasanter to eat than the other, and its flesh seems somewhat firmer.

The Indian Ocean produces Sea-snakes with water-broad tails;
the lakes also produce water snakes of immense; size.
But apparently these snakes in the Ocean bite with teeth that
are saw-like rather than poisonous.

10. The Indian Mule

In India there are herds of wild horses and, wild The Indian asses.

Now they say that when the asses mount the Mule mares, the latter remain passive and take pleasure in the act and produce Mules of a red colour and extremely swift of foot, but that these Mules are impatient of the yoke and generally skittish. The people are said to catch them with foot-traps and then to take them to the King of the Prasii.

If they are caught as two-year-olds they do not refuse to be broken in, but when older they are just as savage as fanged and carnivorous beasts.

They say that among the Prasii in India there is a race of Monkeys with human intelligence; in appearance they are as large as Hyrcanian hounds, and they are seen to possess a natural forelock; anyone who did not know the facts would say that these forelocks were artificial.

The beard that grows beneath their chin is like that of a satyr, while the tail is as long as a lion's. The whole of their body is white except for the head and the tip of the tail, which are red.

They are sober and naturally tame. They live in the forests and feed on wild produce.

They visit the suburbs of Latage (this is a city in India) in great numbers and feed on the boiled rice which the king has served out to them, and this meal is prepared and laid out for them every day.

And when they have eaten their fill, it is said that they withdraw again to their haunts in the forest in an orderly fashion without damaging anything that they come across.

12. The Yak

In India there is a herbivorous animal and it is twice the size of a horse. It has a very bushy tail, pitch-black in colour; the hairs of it are finer than those of man, and Indian women set great store by obtaining them, and in fact they braid them in and adorn themselves most beautifully, plaiting them in with their own hair.

Each hair attains a length of two cubits, and there spring perhaps as many as thirty from one root, like a tassel. Now this is of all animals the most timid, for if it is seen by somebody and realises that it is being looked at, it flees as fast as it can, the pace of its legs only exceeded by its eagerness to escape.

It is hunted by horsemen with swift-footed hounds. But if it realises that it is going to be caught, it hides its tail in some thicket, faces about, and stands waiting for its pursuers and plucks up its courage, fancying that, since its tail is not visible, it will no longer seem worth pursuing.

For it knows that its beauty resides in its tail. And yet on this point its fancies are idle, for a man shoots it with a poisoned arrow and having killed it will cut off its tail, the reward of the chase.

And after flaying the body (for the hide also is serviceable) he leaves the dead carcass, because the Indians have no use for the flesh of these animals.

It seems that in the Indian Ocean there are sea-monsters five times the size of the largest elephant.

At any rate a single rib of a Sea-monsters measures as much as twenty cubits; it has a jaw of fifteen cubits; the fin beside each of the gills is seven cubits in width.

The Trumpet-shells and Purple-shellfish of the Indian Ocean are large enough to contain easily six pints; further, the shells of Sea-urchins have the same capacity.

As for Fishes, they are gigantic, especially the Basse, the Pelamyd, and the Gilthead. And I have heard that at the season when the rivers descend in violence owing to floods and spill themselves upon the land, the Fish also are emptied over the fields and are borne hither and thither in shallow water.

But when the rains which have over-filled the rivers cease, and the streams withdraw again and return to their natural courses, then Fishes of as much as eight cubits long remain in low-lying, marshy, level spots, where what is known as 'fallow land' commonly has depressions.

And the cultivators catch the Fish which can only swim feebly, since they are not moving in deep water but on the surface, glad to snatch a bare existence from the shallow water.

14. The Skate and the prawn of India

Indian fish have the following peculiarities.

The Skate there is as large as an Argolic shield; the prawns of India are even larger than crayfish.

Now these Prawns ascend the river Ganges from the sea and have claws of immense size and, rough to the touch, whereas I learn, that those that quit the Red Sea for the Indus have smooth spines, and the feelers attached to them are long and curly, but they have no claws.

15. The Turtle and the Tortoise of India

The river-Turtle of India c has a shell as large as a full-sized skiff. At any rate each one has a capacity of ten medimni of pulse.

There are also land-Tortoises, and these may be the size of the largest clods of earth which are turned up in deep ploughing, provided the soil is yielding and the plough goes deep and cuts a furrow without difficulty and brings up the clods.

And they say that these Tortoises shed their covering. Now the ploughmen and all who work in the fields dig them out with mattocks and extract them as we extract caterpillars from plants which are worm-eaten.

The flesh of Tortoises is sweet and they are fat and by no means bitter like the Turtles.

16. The Ants of India

In our country also there are intelligent animals but they are few and not so numerous as in India. In that land, for example, are the Elephant, the Parrot, the Sphinx-ape, and the Satyrs, as they are called.

The Indian Ant too, it seems, is a clever creature. True, the Ants of our country excavate their holes and burrow below ground and construct hidden lairs, as it were, by digging in the earth, and wear themselves out with their mysterious and secret mining operations, so to speak.

But the Ants of India construct little houses of material brought together, and these are not in low-lying, level country, which is easily flooded, but high up on rising ground.

And: there with indescribable skill they bore passages and what you might; call Egyptian galleries or Cretan labyrinths and make a place for themselves, not straight ahead or easy to penetrate but out of the way past a maze of tunnels; and on the top they leave a single hole through which they themselves enter and bring into their storehouses all the seeds which they select.

You see, they construct their caves high up in order to escape from inundations and floods from rivers. The result of this clever move is that they are living as it were in watch-towers or on islands at a time when all the land around their hillocks becomes a lake.

Now these mounds, although merely heaped up, are so far from being dissolved and eaten away by an inundation that they are actually strengthened primarily by the morning dew, for they are, so to say, clothed beneath with a fine but strong coating of frost resulting from the dew; then at the base they are bound round with a bark-like coating of weeds from the river mud.

Juba long ago wrote about the Ants of India; but this is all I have to say at present.

17. The Chasm of Pluto

In the country of the Ariani of India there is The chasm a Chasm of Pluto, and at the bottom there are certain mysterious galleries, hidden paths, and passages unseen of man, though they are in fact deep and extend a very long way. But how they came to be and how they were dug, neither the Indians can say nor have I been at the pains to discover. Now the Indians bring to the spot over thirty thousand beasts — sheep, goats, cattle, arid horses.

And everyone who has been scared by some dream or has encountered some omen divine or human, or who has seen some bird in an unfavourable quarter, casts into the Chasm what his personal means can afford by way of ransom for himself, sacrificing the life of an animal for his own life.

And the victims are brought there without being hauled with ropes or otherwise compelled, and make the journey of their own free will owing to some mysterious attraction or spell. Then, as they stand on the brink, of their own accord they leap into the Chasm and are no more seen of the human eye once they have fallen into this mysterious and yawning Chasm of earth, while above are heard the lowing of cattle, the baa of sheep, the neighing of horses, and the bleating of goats.

And anyone, who walks over the surface of the land and comes to the spot and listens, will hear the aforesaid animals for, a very long while. And the confused, sounds never cease, since every day the Indians send in animals for their own redemption.

Now whether it is only the recent victims that are audible or some of the earlier ones also, I cannot say, but audible they are. So much for this singular trait in the animals of that country.

Get All The Books In The Series:

Animal Peculiarity Volume 4 Part 1 [1-3]
Crack Videos
Beautiful gold Frames and prints